TELL ME HOW

How COLD?

by
Azra Limbada

KidHaven PUBLISHING

Published in 2023 by **KidHaven Publishing, an Imprint of Greenhaven Publishing, LLC**
29 East 21st Street
New York, NY 10010

Edited by: William Anthony

Designed by: Danielle Webster-Jones

Cataloging-in-Publication Data

Names: Limbada, Azra.
Title: How cold? / Azra Limbada.
Description: New York : KidHaven Publishing, 2023. | Series: Tell me how | Includes glossary and index.
Identifiers: ISBN 9781534540811 (pbk.) | ISBN 9781534540835 (library bound) | ISBN 9781534540828 (6 pack) | ISBN 9781534540842 (ebook)
Subjects: LCSH: Animals--Arctic regions--Juvenile literature.
Classification: LCC QL105.L563 2023 | DDC 590.911--dc23

Manufactured in the United States of America

CPSIA compliance information: Batch #CSKH23: For further information contact Greenhaven Publishing LLC, New York, New York at 1-844-317-7404.

Please visit our website, www.greenhavenpublishing.com. For a free color catalog of all our high-quality books, call toll free 1-844-317-7404 or fax 1-844-317-7405.

Find us on

Image Credits

Cover – Vaclav Sebek. 4 – Bering Land Bridge National Preserve. 5 – 3Dstock. 6 – bruno pagnanelli. 7 – Volodymyr Goinyk. 8–9 – Eric Isselee, Alexey Seafarer, Kotomiti Okuma. 10 – Ondrej Prosicky. 11 – Giedriius. 12 – Vaclav Sebek. 13 – Sylvie Bouchard. 14 – Vivienstock. 15 – dezy. 16 – Jan Martin Will. 17 – Roger Clark ARPS. 18 – FotoRequest. 19 – Olga Shpak / CC BY-SA (https://creativecommons.org/licenses/by-sa/3.0). 20 – I. Noyan Yilmaz. 21 – Patrick Poendl. 22 – Tarpan. 23 – Big Boy, Sokol Artstudio, MaddyZ, SofiaV, onair. Images are courtesy of Shutterstock.com. With thanks to Getty Images, Thinkstock Photo and iStockphoto.

CONTENTS

Words that look like **this** can be found in the glossary on page 24.

EXTREME ANIMALS

Bowhead whales live in freezing cold waters.

Extremophiles are living things that can survive in **extreme** places. They can live in very harsh conditions, such as in the middle of the freezing ocean!

This is a tardigrade. Tardigrades are tiny. They can survive in the freezing cold or under a rock in a boiling hot desert!

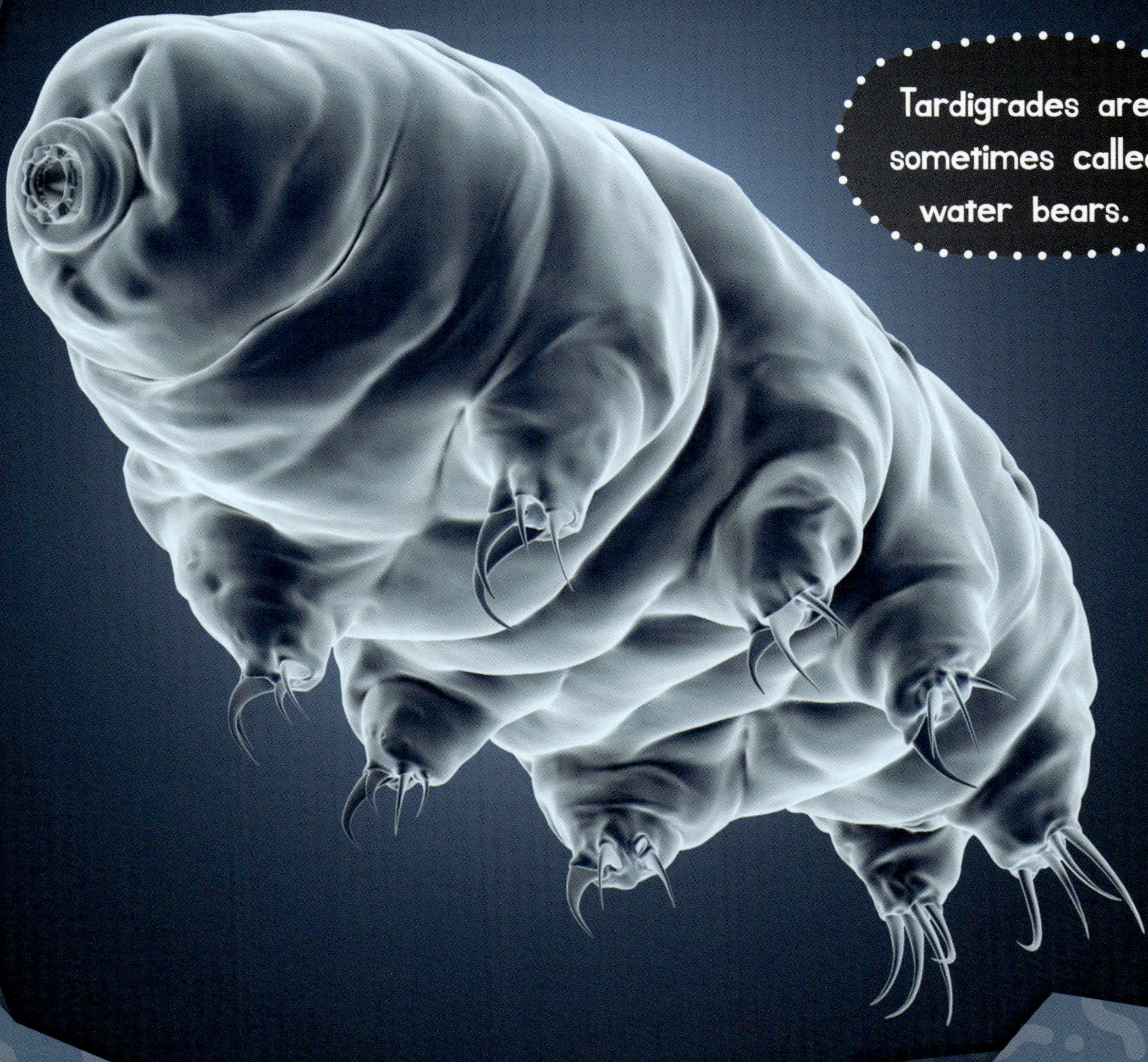

Tardigrades are sometimes called water bears.

LIVING IN THE COLD

The coldest place on Earth is Antarctica. A lot of it is covered in snow. The lowest **temperature** recorded in Antarctica is -144 degrees Fahrenheit (-98 degrees Celsius).

Brr! That is very cold!

Surviving in the cold temperatures in Antarctica is difficult for most animals. Those who can are extremophiles. Lots of these animals are **predators**.

HOW COLD?

These animals all live in very cold temperatures. Some live in the water and some live on the land. They all have different ways of surviving in the cold. Let's see what temperatures these animals can live at.

SEAL
24.8 degrees Fahrenheit (-2 degrees Celsius)

Seals live in Arctic waters. They have special flippers that help them to swim quickly. Seals also have fat under their skin that helps them to float.

POLAR BEAR
-40 degrees Fahrenheit
(-40 degrees Celsius)

SIBERIAN HUSKY
-40 degrees Fahrenheit
(-40 degrees Celsius)

EMPEROR PENGUIN
-76 degrees Fahrenheit
(-60 degrees Celsius)

SEAL

Seals are **mammals** that live mostly in water. There are lots of different types of seals. Seals are **carnivores** and feed on fish, squid, and even seabirds.

A seal's skin is thick and keeps it warm. Seals shed their skin. This means their old skin comes off while new skin grows underneath. Seals shed their skin every year.

POLAR BEAR

Most polar bears live in the freezing Arctic. They have an excellent sense of smell. Polar bears can smell their **prey** from up to 20 miles (32 km) away!

Polar bears are the largest carnivores on land.

Polar bears are covered in layers of fat, called blubber. This helps them stay warm and survive in the freezing Arctic weather.

Polar bears are great swimmers and use their large paws to help them paddle.

SIBERIAN HUSKY

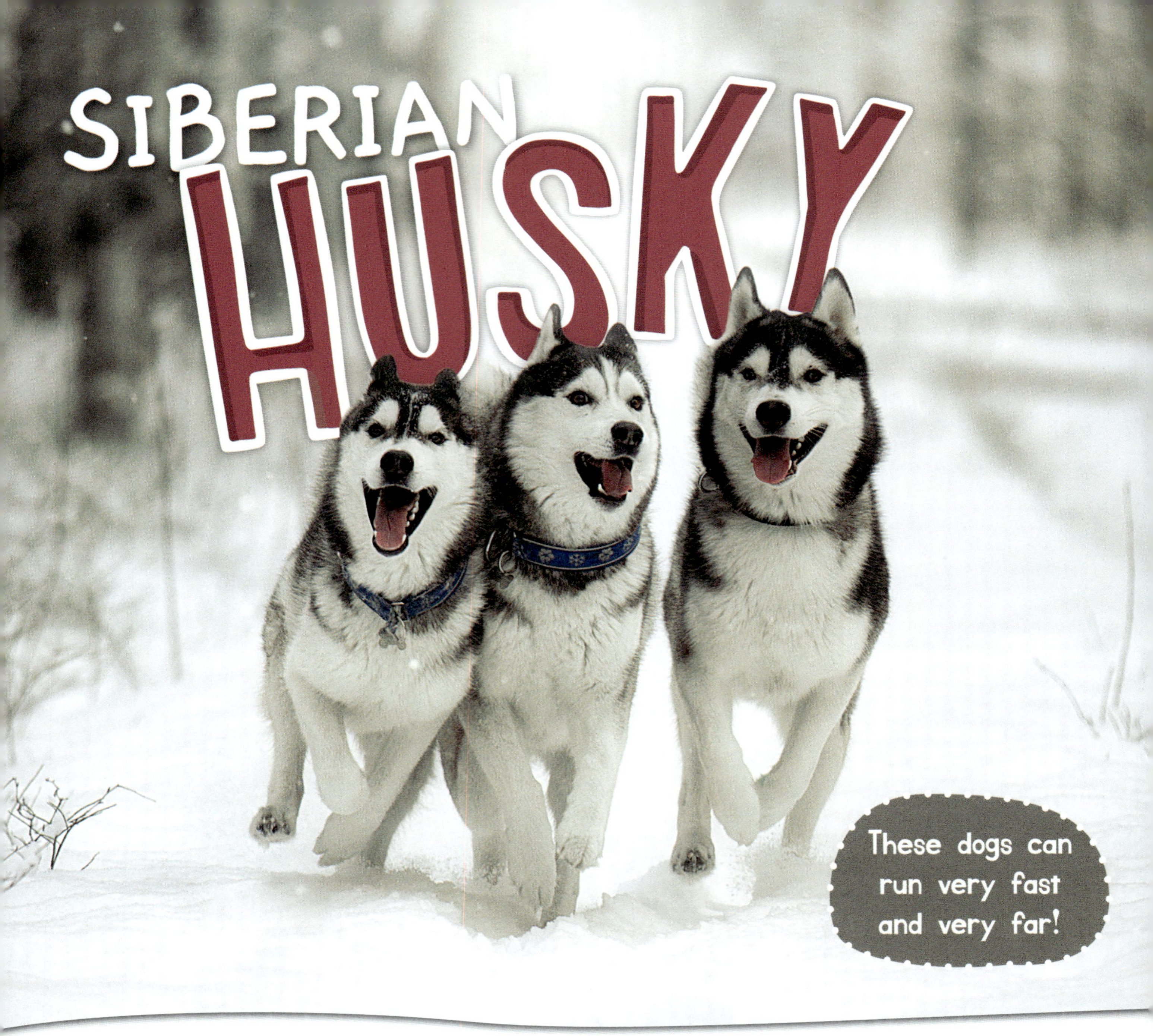

These dogs can run very fast and very far!

A Siberian husky is a type of dog. It comes from a place called Siberia. Huskies are sometimes used to pull a sled through the snow.

Siberia is very cold. Many mammals only have one layer of fur, but Siberian huskies have two. This helps them to stay warm.

Most huskies will shed their fur twice a year.

EMPEROR PENGUIN

The emperor penguin is the largest penguin on Earth. It spends all of its life on the ice or in the freezing waters of Antarctica.

Emperor penguins have strong claws on their feet to help them walk on ice.

Emperor penguins have lots of blubber under their skin to help keep them warm. They also have special feathers that protect them from icy winds.

AMAZING ADAPTATIONS

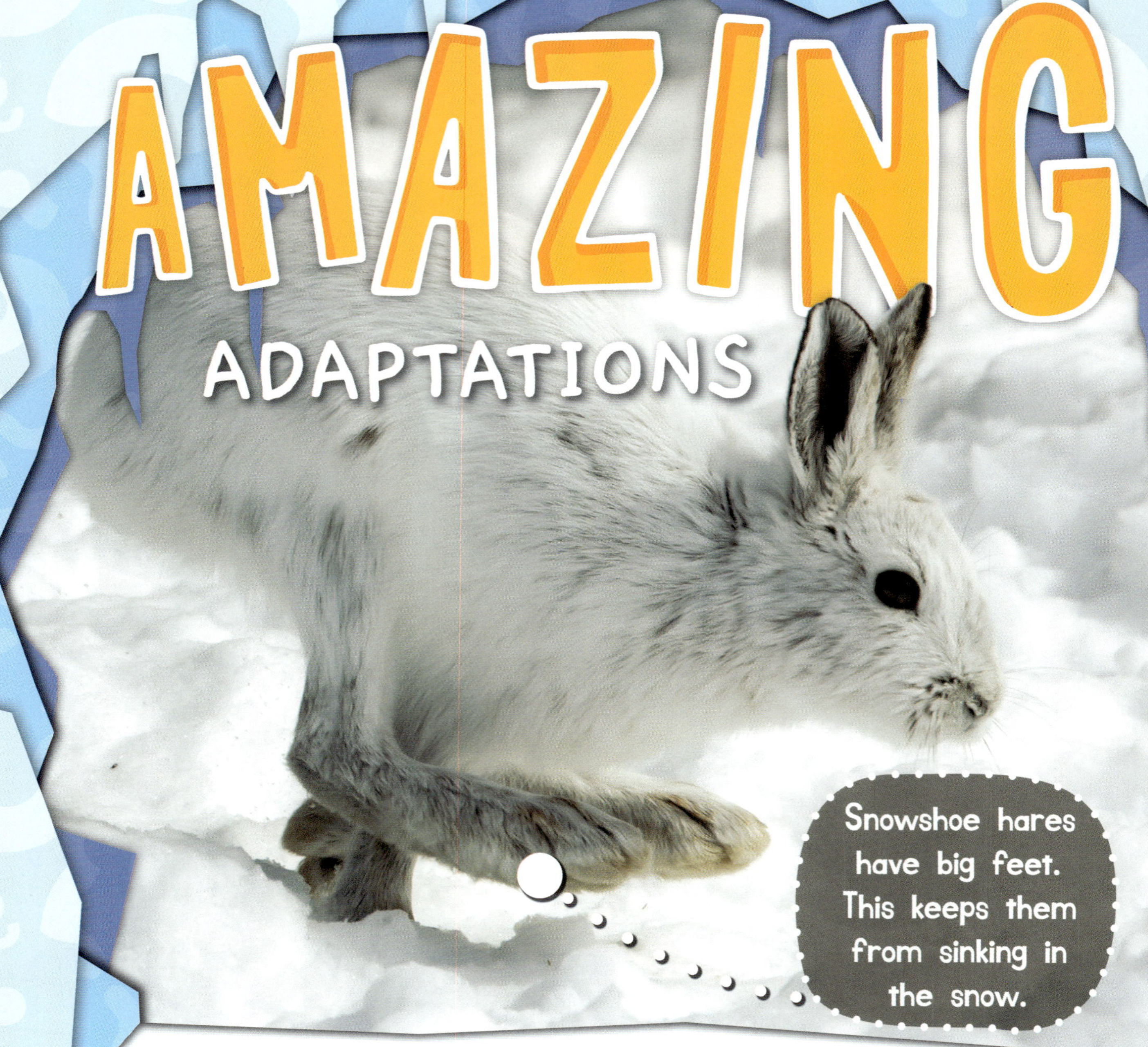

Snowshoe hares have big feet. This keeps them from sinking in the snow.

All animals are adapted to their environment. They have certain **features** that help them to survive in their **habitat**.

A bowhead whale has a big, arched head that helps it break through ice floating on top of the water.

LIFE IN ANTARCTICA

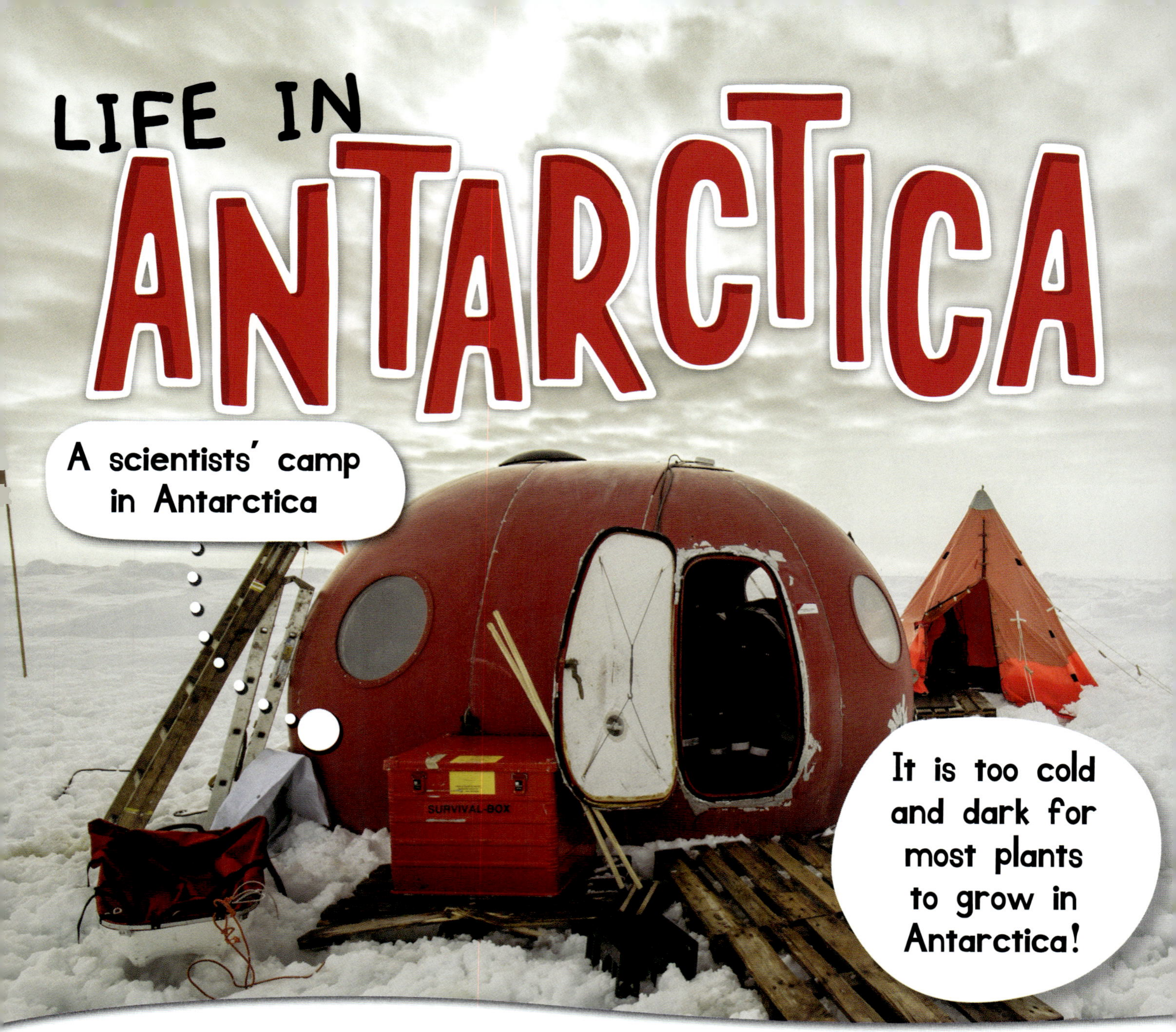

Antarctica is too cold for people to live there all the time. Most people only visit Antarctica in the summer months.

Antarctica only has two seasons – winter and summer. The summer season is bright and sunny, but the winter season is very dark.

Do you think you could live in Antarctica?

CREATE A CREATURE

A snow petrel is a bird that can be found in Antarctica. It is white like snow. This helps it **camouflage** in its habitat.

It's your turn to draw a creature! Think of how it might be adapted to living in a very cold place and label all the different parts!

Tip: Give your creature a special name!

Remember to explain how your creature can survive!

GLOSSARY

Arctic the area of the world that includes the North Pole

camouflage to blend into your surroundings

carnivores animals that eat other animals instead of plants

extreme far beyond what is usual or normal

features interesting or important parts

habitat the natural home in which animals, plants, and other living things live

mammals animals that are warm-blooded, have a backbone, and produce milk to feed their children

predators animals that hunt other animals for food

prey an animal that is hunted, caught, and eaten by another animal

temperature how hot or cold something is

INDEX